HARDEST
OF HISTORY

Warriors

TRACEY TURNER

ILLUSTRATED BY JAMIE LENMAN

A & C BLACK
AN IMPRINT OF BLOOMSBURY
LONDON NEW DELHI NEW YORK SYDNEY

First published 2014 by
A & C Black, an imprint of Bloomsbury Publishing Plc
50 Bedford Square, London WC1B 3DP

www.bloomsbury.com

Bloomsbury is a registered trademark of Bloomsbury Publishing Plc

ISBN 978-1-4729-0564-2

A CIP catalogue for this book is available from the British Library.

Printed in China by Leo Paper Products, Heshan, Guangdong

1 3 5 7 9 10 8 6 4 2

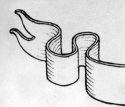

CONTENTS

PLACES TO CONQUER

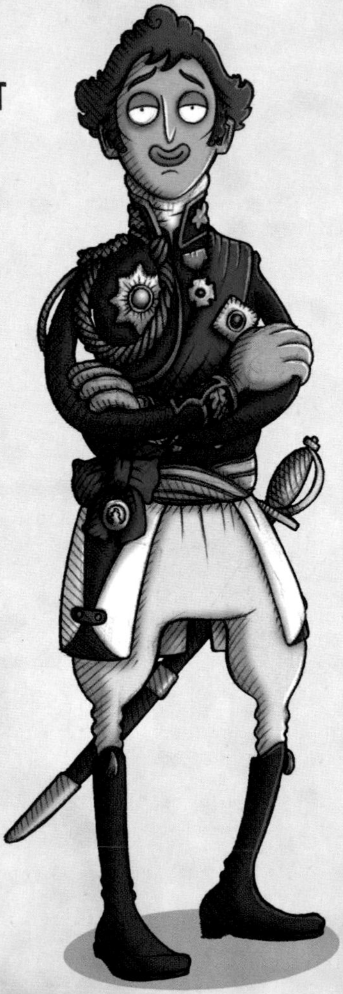

INTRODUCTION

This book contains some of the hardest warriors of all time, from conquering medieval kings to brilliant Roman generals. Some of them were brave, some were ruthless, and others were wickedly clever. But all of them were as hard as nails.

FIND OUT ABOUT . . .

- The conqueror whose skull ended up as a cup

- A pair of rebel sisters who ruled Vietnam

- The British prime minister who fought in a duel

- A female samurai warrior

If you've ever wanted to ride a war elephant or fire a trebuchet, read on. Follow the hard nuts through a freezing Russian winter, across the Rubicon River, and into the mountains of Mexico.

As well as discovering stories of courage and cunning, you might be in for a few surprises. Did you know, for example, that the Ming Dynasty was started by a starving peasant? Or that Cyrus the Great commanded soldiers mounted on dromedary camels?

You're about to meet some of the toughest warriors in history . . .

Plus play the game on page 36 and see if you've got what it takes to conqueror an enormous empire!

CYRUS THE GREAT

Cyrus the Great was a warrior king with a talent for conquering. He founded the mighty Persian Empire, the largest of its time.

HARD NUT RATING: 8.3

BASHING THE MEDIANS

When Cyrus became King of Persia in 559 BC, Persia was part of the Median Empire. Cyrus didn't like being ruled by the Median leader, Astyages (or anyone else for that matter) and rebelled. He defeated Astyages and captured the capital city of Ectatana. Now Cyrus was the ruler of the Median Empire, which he liked much better.

BATTERING THE LYDIANS

Croesus, King of Lydia, was worried that Cyrus was becoming too powerful and made the mistake of marching his army against him. Cyrus defeated him at the Battle of Sardis, using

CONQUERING LIST

soldiers mounted on dromedary camels, which frightened the Lydian horses. He ordered King Croesus to be burned to death (though there are stories he might have thought better of it in the end), and added Lydia to his realm.

KING OF THE WORLD

Next on Cyrus's conquering list was the Elam civilisation, followed by Babylonia – both of which Cyrus dealt with swiftly and with a minimum of fuss, but quite a bit of bloodshed. Afterwards he modestly declared himself King of Babylon, King of Sumer and Akkad, and King of the Four Corners of the World. Which wasn't actually that much of an exaggeration.

MESSING WITH THE MASSAGETAE

Cyrus realised that the Massagetae, just to the north of his great empire, remained unconquered. That would never do. Cyrus tried an unusual tactic: he asked its leader, Tomyris, to marry him. Wisely, she refused. So there was nothing for it but to batter the Massagetae Army into submission. But Cyrus was in for a big shock: the Persians were defeated, and Cyrus was killed. The story goes that Queen Tomyris used his skull as a cup to drink out of (see page 42).

MIGHTY EMPIRE

Cyrus had conquered a territory that stretched all the way from the Mediterranean to what's now Pakistan, and founded an empire that would last more than two hundred years. His son, Cambyses II, conquered Egypt and made the Persian Empire even bigger.

HARDOMETER

CUNNING: 9
COURAGE: 9
SURVIVAL SKILLS: 6
RUTHLESSNESS: 9

BABUR

Babur was a warrior who fought for and conquered his own empire – the Moghul Empire in India.

HARD NUT
RATING: 8.5

KICKED OUT

Babur's ancestors included both Genghis Khan and Timur (see pages 12 and 52). With relatives like that, it was no surprise that he took up conquering. Babur became ruler of Farghana in 1495 when he was 12, an area that's now in Uzbekistan. His uncles did their best to kick him off the throne, and he was forced to live in exile. But Babur didn't let them stop him from conquering.

SEIZING SAMARKAND

Two years later, after a long siege, Babur captured the city that his father had tried to capture for years: Samarkand. Feeling confident, he marched on Farghana to take up his throne – but his army was defeated. To make matters worse, the troops he'd left behind in newly captured Samarkand were attacked and defeated while he was away. Babur was left with nothing.

CAPTURING KABUL

In 1504, now a 21-year-old with a strong army, Babur captured the city of Kabul (in what's now Afghanistan) and gained a new and wealthy kingdom. This was more like it. Babur fought his old enemies, the Uzbeks. He had to crush a rebellion in Kabul, and was eventually driven out of the city by revolting generals. But eventually he recaptured the city.

TIMUR

GENGHIS KHAN

INVADING INDIA

Babur began making raids into India in 1519, keeping a greedy eye on its land and wealth. He made more raids over the next few years, but didn't stay in India until his victory at the Battle of Panipat, against the Sultan of Delhi, in 1526. He captured Delhi and marched to Agra. Babur was now surrounded by hostile enemies, but he managed to defeat them and conquer an Indian empire.

MOGHUL EMPIRE

Babur's Indian empire covered most of northern India, with its capital at Agra. His son and grandson made the Moghul Empire even larger, and the Moghuls ruled their empire for more than 300 years after he died.

HARDOMETER

CUNNING: 9
COURAGE: 8
SURVIVAL SKILLS: 9
RUTHLESSNESS: 8

GENGHIS KHAN

Genghis Khan led a rampaging horseback army in Mongolia and beyond, and conquered an empire that became the second largest in the history of the world.

HARD NUT RATING: 8.5

A BAD BEGINNING

Genghis Khan was born in the Gobi desert in Mongolia around 1162. He was the son of the tribe's chief, but when he was nine his father was murdered, and Genghis and the rest of his family were cast out of the tribe. Things got even worse when a different tribe captured Genghis and held him prisoner – but he made a daring escape and earned a reputation for bravery in the process.

MONGOLS UNITED

Genghis married the daughter of another tribal chief, and his powerful new family and hard-nut reputation earned him followers. He soon discovered he liked being in charge, and decided to unite the tribes of Mongolia, which were constantly fighting one another, and put himself in charge of all of them.

HARDOMETER

CUNNING: 8
COURAGE: 8
SURVIVAL SKILLS: 9
RUTHLESSNESS: 9

UNIVERSAL LEADER

Genghis managed to persuade or bully the different Mongol tribes into uniting. Sometimes he was a bit heavy handed – when one tribe wouldn't do as he wanted, he killed all the adult tribespeople. By 1206 all the Mongolian tribes were united, and he was given the name Genghis Khan, which means 'Universal Leader' (until then he'd been called Temujin).

CONQUERING

Genghis formed a tough, disciplined, horseback-mounted army from the united Mongol tribes: they were deadly accurate archers and fearsome warriors. Genghis led them on a conquering spree, starting with northwestern China, and continuing into other parts of Central Asia, Russia and India.

EXPANDING EMPIRE

Genghis and his Mongolian army were extremely successful. His empire stretched all the way from modern-day Poland and Turkey in the west, to southeast Asia and the coast of China in the east. After he died in 1227, Genghis's descendants made the empire even bigger led by his grandson Kublai Khan. It was the second biggest empire ever (the biggest was the British Empire in the 20th century).

THE TRUNG SISTERS

Vietnamese heroines the Trung sisters rebelled against their Chinese rulers, and ended up running the country.

HARD NUT
RATING: 7.8

CHINESE RULERS

Vietnam was ruled by the Chinese Han Dynasty by the time the Trung sisters, Trung Trac and Trung Nhi, were born, around AD 10. Their father was a powerful lord, and they grew up in a time when Vietnamese women were allowed to become leaders, warriors, business women and judges. The sisters studied martial arts, and grew up tough.

INCITING A REBELLION

Foreign rule was bad enough, but when the Chinese executed Trung Trac's husband, the Trung sisters decided to do something about it, and persuaded the Vietnamese lords to start a rebellion against the Chinese. The story goes that the sisters performed daring deeds to show how hard they were. One of these daring deeds included killing a fierce man-eating tiger, and writing a proclamation on its skin telling everyone to rise up against their foreign rulers.

REBEL ARMY

The Trung sisters must have been very persuasive, because they ended up with an army of 80,000 soldiers, who were trained to be fearsome warriors, including 36 women the Trungs chose to be army generals. Then the army marched against the Chinese, with the Trung sisters bravely leading the way. They captured 65 cities held by the Chinese, and drove their enemies out of Vietnam in AD 40.

TRUNGS IN CHARGE

The people of Vietnam celebrated the victory, and proclaimed the Trung sisters as joint queens. They ruled Vietnam for the next few years. Not surprisingly, the Chinese weren't pleased that they'd been thrown out of Vietnam by a couple of women, and attacked the country to try and win it back. No matter how bravely and fiercely the Trungs and the Vietnamese fought, the Chinese army was bigger and better equipped. In AD 43 the Chinese finally won.

EVADING CAPTURE

Instead of being captured by the Chinese, the Trung sisters chose to kill themselves. One legend says that they drowned themselves. The sisters became national heroes, and are still remembered in poems, songs and art.

HARDOMETER

CUNNING: 8
COURAGE: 9
SURVIVAL SKILLS: 6
RUTHLESSNESS: 8

TOUGH-NUT WOMEN

Most really famous hard nuts are men, but there are plenty of rock-hard women as well. Boudica, Joan of Arc, Tomyris, Tomoe Gozen and the Trung sisters are all in this book but below is a look at a few more tough-nut females from throughout history.

ARTEMESIA

Artemesia was Queen of Halicarnassos. Today it's in Turkey, but in the 400s BC it was part of the Persian Empire. Persian emperor Xerxes I invaded Greece, and fought the Greeks in a famous sea battle at Salamis. Artemesia commanded her own fleet of five ships for the Persians, and put all the male Persian commanders to shame with her skill and bravery.

CLEOPATRA

Cleopatra ruled Egypt with her younger brother but was kicked out because she wanted to rule on her own. With the help of a powerful Roman boyfriend, Julius Caesar, she got rid of her brother. After Caesar died, Cleopatra made a brave attempt at grabbing the entire Roman Empire, by declaring that her son with Caesar was the true heir to the empire. Her plan, hatched with another Roman boyfriend, didn't work out. She killed herself by letting a venomous snake bite her.

ZENOBIA

Zenobia was Queen of Palmyra in Syria. In AD 269 she conquered Egypt, and went on to conquer a big bit of Anatolia (in what's now Turkey) and chunks of land in the Middle East. She was known as a brilliant horse-rider and a brave warrior. The Romans finally defeated her in battle and captured Zenobia, despite her daring escape by camel.

GRACE O'MALLEY

Grace was an Irish leader who controlled her coastline by becoming a pirate in the 1500s. She was ruthless and brave, and grew wealthy from her seafaring. She also defeated her English enemies, pouring hot lead on their heads when they attacked her castle.

FLORA SANDES

Flora was one of only two British woman to fight in the First World War. She joined an ambulance service and was sent to Serbia, where she enlisted in the Serbian army (there were a few other Serbian women soldiers too). Flora was wounded in 1916 and received a medal for bravery.

KING PIYE

Piye was a warrior king who invaded and conquered Egypt, and founded a new Egyptian dynasty.

HARD NUT RATING: 9

KUSHY

Piye was king of a kingdom to the south of Egypt, called Kush, in the 700s BC. In ancient times Kush was part of Nubia (today it would be in Sudan). Hundreds of years before Piye was King of Kush, the whole of Egypt had been ruled by powerful pharaohs, but now Egypt was split into different territories, ruled by different leaders.

CONQUERING UPPER EGYPT

King Piye had a perfectly good kingdom of his own, but the fertile lands of Egypt were not far away, and he couldn't resist paying the country a visit. And he took his army with him. It wasn't long before he'd conquered Upper Egypt – the southern part of the country. Piye's sister was accepted as a priestess of the god Amun Re, who was worshipped by the Kushites as well as the Egyptians. The role was political as well as religious, and meant that Piye now controlled even more land.

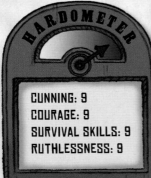

HARDOMETER

CUNNING: 9
COURAGE: 9
SURVIVAL SKILLS: 9
RUTHLESSNESS: 9

DELTA ALLIANCE

At the Nile Delta in Lower Egypt, where the River Nile meets the Mediterranean Sea, there were several different leaders. One of them in particular, Tefnakht, didn't like Piye's conquering – he was becoming far too powerful for Tefnakht's liking.

So he got together with a group of the other Nile Delta leaders and formed an army against the Kushite King.

CONQUERING LOWER EGYPT

Piye was having none of it. He marched north and defeated the allied leaders' army. Just to show everyone he really was in charge, he captured cities in the north of Egypt, including Memphis, the ancient Egyptian capital. Now he had conquered Lower Egypt as well as Upper Egypt.

PIYE RULES

The Nile Delta leaders admitted they were beaten, and accepted that Piye was now in control of their lands – apart from Tefnakht, who ran away. Piye was in charge of Egypt until he died in 716 BC. He never became pharaoh of Egypt, but his son succeeded him and he did become pharaoh, starting a new Kushite dynasty.

GERONIMO

Geronimo was a fearless Apache warrior who gained a fearsome reputation from his enemies.

HARD NUT RATING: 8.3

INDIANS VS SETTLERS

Geronimo was part of a group of Native American Apache Indians, who lived in what's now the state of Arizona in the United States. By the time he was born, in 1829, Europeans had already been settled in the United States for hundreds of years, and the Native Americans were being moved out of their homelands. Some Native Americans, including Geronimo's group of Apaches, made raids on the settlers to try and drive them out, and the settlers fought back.

RAIDERS

Geronimo was away trading when a group of Mexican soldiers raided his camp. When he returned with the other men, they found that many of the women and children had been murdered, including Geronimo's mother, wife and three children. After that, Geronimo's attacks on the Mexicans became more frequent and more violent and he soon earned a reputation as a fearless warrior. One story says he braved a hail of bullets to attack Mexican soldiers with a knife. He became leader of his group of Apache warriors.

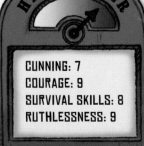

HARDOMETER

CUNNING: 7
COURAGE: 9
SURVIVAL SKILLS: 8
RUTHLESSNESS: 9

APACHE RESERVATION

In 1874, thousands of Apaches were moved off their land and onto a reservation in Arizona by the United States government. The land was barren and the people were miserable. Hundreds of them followed Geronimo out of the reservation and became outlaws, continuing their war against the settlers. But eventually, in 1884, Geronimo surrendered.

ESCAPE

In 1885, Geronimo ran away from the reservation again, but he was tracked by the United States Army in Mexico, and surrendered. As they approached the border to the United States, Geronimo was worried that his Apache band of warriors would be killed once they were in United States territory – and so he made another bid to escape!

CAPTURED AGAIN

More than 5000 men set off in pursuit of Geronimo and his small band. After five months, the Apaches were tracked down to their camp in Mexico. Geronimo was persuaded to surrender again, and he was promised that he could soon return to Arizona. It wasn't true. First Geronimo was imprisoned, then he was sent to a new reservation in Oklahoma. But Geronimo's fighting days were over. He lived peacefully, and wrote a book about his life.

JULIUS CAESAR

Julius Caesar is one of the most famous warriors of all time. His military conquests helped make him the most powerful person in the ancient Roman world.

HARD NUT RATING: 8.3

EXILE AND HOMECOMING

Caesar was born into a wealthy Roman family in 100 BC, but was forced to live in exile because the brutal Roman dictator, Sulla, was an old family enemy and was busy executing anyone he didn't like in Rome. When he returned to Rome after Sulla's death, Caesar's charm and tough-nut reputation won him several top jobs in politics. As governor of Spain, Caesar led his troops in an invasion of what's now Portugal, which was very successful and made him even more popular. The Romans were very keen on conquering heroes.

GALLIC WARS

Even though Julius Caesar now held the most important job in Rome, he wasn't happy. He seized power with two friends, Pompey and Crassus. Then he went off to Gaul (modern-day France and Belgium) for a spot of conquering. It took him eight years, but he succeeded in conquering all of it, and adding a huge chunk to the empire, along with lots of treasure and slaves. He was so pleased with his conquests that he wrote a book about his time in Gaul, *The Gallic Wars*.

CIVIL WAR

The three-man leadership of Rome didn't work out. Crassus was killed, and Caesar fell out with Pompey. They fought each other over who should be in charge of Rome. The politicians backed Pompey, but Caesar had the advantage of an army, brilliant battle tactics and a single-minded lust for power. He crossed the Rubicon River, marched on Rome, met Pompey at the Battle of Pharsalus and won, even though his troops were outnumbered by Pompey's.

STABBED

After his victory, Caesar was made Dictator of the Empire for a period of ten years. But then Caesar went one step further – he made himself Dictator for Life. He was extremely popular because of his conquering skills, but not *that* popular. Many people in Rome thought he'd taken too much power for himself, and a group of Roman politicians decided to do something about it and stabbed him to death.

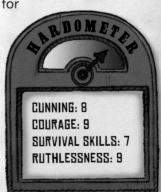

HARDOMETER

CUNNING: 8
COURAGE: 9
SURVIVAL SKILLS: 7
RUTHLESSNESS: 9

THE DUKE OF WELLINGTON

HARD NUT RATING: 8.3

Wellington is one of Britain's best generals. He's most famous for defeating the French revolutionary leader, Napoleon, at Waterloo.

BRITISH ARMY

Wellington was born in Dublin in 1769, to rich, Anglo-Irish parents. He joined the British Army in 1787 and fought in India, where he won a series of victories and earned a reputation as a brilliant general who commanded his troops with firm discipline.

NAPOLEONIC WARS

In 1808 Wellington commanded the British, Portuguese and Spanish Armies in the Peninsula War. The war was part of a bigger conflict – the Napoleonic Wars. This was fought between France, which had recently had a revolution, and other countries in Europe, who were very keen not to have revolutions themselves, and who also wanted to put things in France back to the way they were before (with a king and aristocratic people in charge). Coming from a wealthy and upper class background, Wellington wholeheartedly agreed. He drove the French Army out of Portugal and Spain, and became a British hero.

WATERLOO

In 1814, Napoleon was exiled to the island of Elba in the Mediterranean Sea. Wellington, meanwhile, was made a Duke back in Britain (before that he'd just been Arthur Wellesley). But in 1815 Napoleon escaped from his island and raised an army in France. Wellington set off immediately at the head of the British Army, and met Napoleon at the Battle of Waterloo in Belgium. Wellington had the help of the Prussian Army, and through a series of clever battle tactics defeated the French for good. Napoleon was exiled again (somewhere much further away this time), and Wellington became even more of a hero to the British.

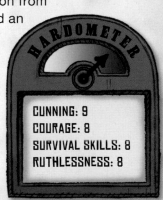

PRIME MINISTER

At the same time as being a top British general, Wellington was also a politician. Once he'd won the Battle of Waterloo he concentrated on politics, and became Prime Minister in 1828. But that didn't stop Wellington from fighting completely. In 1829 he had an argument with another politician, Lord Winchelsea, and decided that the only way to resolve the issue was by a duel with pistols in Battersea Park. They both missed – on purpose – but honour was maintained.

HARDOMETER

CUNNING: 9
COURAGE: 8
SURVIVAL SKILLS: 8
RUTHLESSNESS: 8

MAHMUD OF GHAZNI

Mahmud was a hard nut warrior who expanded the Ghaznavid Empire and relentlessly raided India.

HARD NUT RATING: 8

GRABBING THE THRONE

Mahmud was born in 971 in what's now southeastern Afghanistan. His father died in 997, having conquered the empire of Ghazni. Mahmud was away when he heard about his father's death, and he was absolutely furious when he learned that his father had named his younger brother, Ismail, as heir. Mahmud wasn't having it. He marched east, captured the capital city of Ghazni, made himself king and put his younger brother under house arrest for life.

GHAZNI GETS BIGGER

Mahmud wasn't happy with his empire as it was. He thought it needed to be quite a lot bigger and so set off with his horse cavalry and archers on a path of conquest, adding new lands in Central and South Asia to the Ghaznavid Empire. By 1001, he'd conquered an impressive amount. But it still wasn't quite big enough for Mahmud.

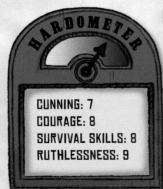

HARDOMETER

CUNNING: 7
COURAGE: 8
SURVIVAL SKILLS: 8
RUTHLESSNESS: 9

RAIDING INDIA

Mahmud had his eye on India, and in 1001 he made the first of many raids into the Punjab, home of the fierce Rajputs. His quick cavalry outmanoeuvred the elephant-mounted Rajput warriors, and Mahmud added chunks of northern India to his growing empire. Over the next

30 years he made no fewer than 17 raids into northern India. Each time, Mahmud and his army returned home before the monsoon came and blocked their path back to Ghazni.

MAKING ENEMIES

As time went on, the relentless raiding and killing continued, but with extra looting because Mahmud's empire was in need of more funds. Mahmud ruthlessly targeted Hindu temples and stole the gold. In 1025 he captured Somnath, and destroyed its beautiful temple. Fifty thousand people died defending Somnath, making Mahmud one of the most hated Hindu enemies ever.

GREAT GHAZNAVID EMPIRE

At the same time as fighting, Mahmud also encouraged learning, and he made Ghazni into one of the cultural centres of the world. When he died in 1030 his empire stretched from what's now Afghanistan, through Central Asia to Pakistan, and through northern India to the Indian Ocean on the coast of Gujarat. The empire was ruled by Mahmud's successors for more than 150 years.

THE WORLD'S WORST WARS

All wars are pretty dreadful. They are full of violence, blood, loud noises, and of course, death. One of the worst wars in history was the Second World War. Seventy million people died – the highest number of deaths of any war. Here are three other particularly bloody and unpleasant conflicts from throughout history.

THE NAPOLEONIC WARS

After the French Revolution, lots of European countries were at war with France. The French leader, Napoleon, led France to victory and defeat during this time – the most famous of these is the Battle of Waterloo. The worst part of the Napoleonic Wars was the attack on Russia in 1812. Napoleon led an invasion force of 650,000 soldiers. They followed the Russian Army, who burned everything behind them as they went so that there was no food or shelter for the French. The bitterly cold Russian winter froze the exhausted, hungry French troops, who were attacked and defeated by the Russians. Only 40,000 French soldiers made it back to France.

THE RUSSIAN CIVIL WAR

After the Russian Revolution, which ended up with the Bolsheviks in charge, Russia had an absolutely massive civil war (1918-21). As well as the Russian people involved on each side, other countries joined the opposition to the Bolsheviks because they didn't want revolutionaries in control, and formed the White Army. Bolshevik supporters formed the Red Army. If either side took prisoners, they were usually executed. The Red Army killed 50,000 White Army prisoners of war and civilians after they'd surrendered in one of the worst massacres of the civil war. After the war, Russia was in such a terrible state that millions starved.

THE FIRST WORLD WAR

The First World War (1914-18) was fought between Britain, France and their allies, and Germany and its allies. Powerful new guns gouged enormous holes in the landscape, forcing the soldiers to take cover in trenches, which were often muddy, cramped and full of rats. Battles had extremely high death tolls – on the first day of the Battle of the Somme, there were 60,000 dead and wounded British soldiers. Altogether around 18 million people died in the First World War, and another 21 million were wounded.

JOAN OF ARC

Joan of Arc didn't look like a warrior – she looked like a teenage farm girl – yet she led the entire French army to victory.

HARD NUT RATING: 7

HUNDRED YEARS WAR

When Joan was born, around 1412, a long, bitter war was going on over who should be in control of France. On one side were the Burgundians, who were English allies, and on the other side were supporters of Charles the Dauphin, who claimed the French throne. One half of Joan's village was controlled by the Burgundians, and the other half by Charles' supporters.

VOICES FROM GOD

Joan started hearing voices when she was about 13. She believed they belonged to Christian saints, who began to make some very difficult demands. They told her to help Charles the Dauphin and get rid of the Burgundians. This was a bit tricky for a farmer's daughter, but Joan felt she had to try and do what her voices told her.

JOAN THE KNIGHT

Incredible though it might seem, Joan managed to get a meeting with Charles, and then to persuade him that he needed her help. She was dressed as a knight, put on a horse, and sent off to fight at the city of Orleans, which was besieged by the English and their allies. Even though she'd never fought

HARDOMETER

CUNNING: 7
COURAGE: 9
SURVIVAL SKILLS: 5
RUTHLESSNESS: 7

in a war before, Joan became a heroine almost overnight. She fought bravely and cleverly, and the English were sent packing. For her part in the victory, Joan was put in charge of the entire French Army, alongside the Duke of Alençon.

KING CHARLES

Joan seemed to have a knack for leading an army. She led the French against the Burgundians, chasing them out of one town after another and defeating them in battle. The French did so well that Charles was crowned King of France.

CAPTURE

In 1430 Joan was captured by the Burgundians. She escaped twice, but finally stood trial at a church court in 1431. The court found Joan guilty of being a witch, and she met a terrible end when she was burned at the stake. She's now a saint in the Catholic Church.

HONGWU

Hongwu fought his way from starving peasant to powerful warlord, and finally emperor of the whole of China.

HARD NUT RATING: 9

A HARD LIFE

When Hongwu was born in 1328, the Yuan dynasty ruled China – the dynasty had begun with Genghis Khan's grandson, Kublai Khan. For peasants like Hongwu, life was hard – there was widespread drought and famine, and millions of people died of starvation. Rebel peasant bands formed, and robbed rich families and shared what they'd stolen among the poor (like Chinese Robin Hoods).

THE RED TURBANS

Hongwu joined a rebel band known as the Red Turbans, led by Guo Zixing. Hongwu was tough and clever, and quickly rose to be second-in-command of Guo's rebel army. He captured cities and expanded the rebel army, and when Guo died in 1355, Hongwu took over as leader.

CHINESE LEADER

After a lot more fighting, Hongwu's empire grew. He captured the important and wealthy city of Nanjing, and used it as his base. Rather than just a rebel leader, he said he was the leader of the whole Chinese nation against the Yuan, and other rebel leaders either submitted to him or were killed. But there were some rebel leaders who wanted

HARDOMETER

CUNNING: 9
COURAGE: 9
SURVIVAL SKILLS: 9
RUTHLESSNESS: 9

to rule China too, and one of them was Chen Youliang, who ruled a large chunk of central China. In 1363 Hongwu fought him in a three-day battle on Lake Poyanghe. Hongwu won, Chen died and his large fleet was destroyed. Hongwu took over Chen's territory and captured other provinces.

MIGHTY MING

Now Hongwu had control of most of the south of China. He sent two of his generals to lead his army against the north, and in 1368 proclaimed himself emperor of a new dynasty – the Ming. He took the name Hongwu, meaning 'vastly martial' (before that he'd been plain old Zhu Yuanzhang). Eleven years later he finally controlled the whole of China, plus Korea for good measure. Hongwu ruled as emperor for 30 years, but he was suspicious of people plotting against him, and had thousands executed. After he died, the Ming Dynasty lasted until 1644.

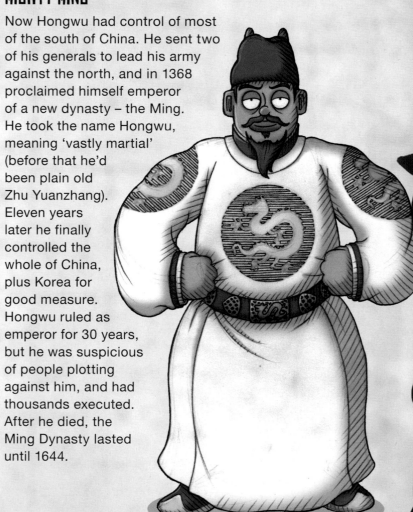

ALEXANDER THE GREAT

HARD NUT RATING: 8.3

Alexander the Great was King of Macedonia, and very quickly became the ruler of a vast empire. He led a conquering army that was never defeated.

KING OF MACEDONIA

The kingdom of Macedonia had risen to be the most powerful nation in the ancient Greek world, and had an empire that included most of Greece. Alexander became its king in 336 BC, when he was 20 years old. His father had been murdered, and Alexander lost no time in killing his father's assassins, along with anyone he felt was a rival to his leadership. When the Greek city-state of Thebes dared to revolt against Macedonian rule, Alexander destroyed the city, killed thousands and sold everyone else into slavery. Now everyone knew it was a mistake to mess with Alexander.

POUNDING THE PERSIANS

Alexander had plans to expand his territory, and he had his eye on the huge Persian Empire – the largest empire in the

PLACES TO CONQUER

world at the time. He attacked the Persian Army in Asia Minor (modern-day Turkey), then Persian lands in the Mediterranean and Egypt. Over the course of several battles, he utterly defeated the Persian leader, Darius III, even though in one battle Alexander's army was half the size of the Persians'. King Darius ran away, and Alexander was proclaimed King of Asia. Then he conquered Susa, the capital of Persia, and Babylon, so that he was in control of the whole Persian Empire.

ALEXANDER'S UNBEATABLE ARMY

Alexander now had a taste for conquering, and he was very good at it. He continued eastwards, capturing new land as he went. He travelled thousands of kilometres into Central Asia, and continued further into what's now Pakistan and India, where he defeated King Poros and his war elephants. The battles fought by Alexander's army always ended in victory. By the time he'd finished conquering, Alexander had founded more than 70 cities.

SUDDEN ENDING

Finally, Alexander turned back, celebrating his victories, massive amounts of treasure, and an empire that now stretched from the Mediterranean to the Himalayas. After an especially big celebration in Babylon, Alexander died suddenly, aged just 32. In the 12 years of his rule, he'd conquered an empire that covered most of the known world, more than three million square kilometres. After his death, Alexander's generals took over different parts of the empire.

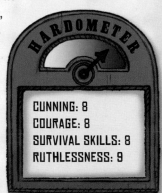

CUNNING: 8
COURAGE: 8
SURVIVAL SKILLS: 8
RUTHLESSNESS: 9

WAR GAME

For two to six players. You'll need a counter each and a dice to play this game.

BEGIN YOUR PATH OF DESTRUCTION HERE.

2

Attack and capture an enemy fortress. Go forward three squares.

12

Ambushed by hostile tribes. Go back two squares.

10

13

Defeated in battle. Go back two squares.

15

16

24

23

Besieged by enemy troops. Miss a go.

Mortally wounded in battle. Go back to the start.

Capture new territory, and loot tons of treasure. Throw again.

27

You're fierce and fearless warriors and in the mood for a punch-up! You're hell bent on conquering as much land and terrifying as many people as possible. But which of you will be hard enough to conquer a massive empire?

4

Disease ravages your troops. Go back three squares.

6

EXILE

Forced into exile by power-hungry relatives. Miss a go.

Brilliant military tactics defeat the enemy. Go forward two squares.

9

18

Win a historic victory. Throw again.

Miss a go while you crush a rebellion.

21

Capture the enemy's capital city. Go forward four squares.

Another glorious victory over your foes. Go forward two squares.

29

Congratulations! You have conquered a vast empire. Now you just have to avoid assassination.

BOUDICA

After the ancient Romans invaded Britain, some brave Britons rebelled against them. One of them was the fierce warrior queen, Boudica.

HARD NUT RATING: 7.5

ROTTEN ROMANS

Boudica was Queen of the Iceni tribe, in what's now East Anglia. The Romans had allowed her husband, King Prastagus, to carry on ruling the tribe after they had invaded. But when Prastagus died, in around AD 60, they decided to take control themselves. They attacked Boudica and her daughters, and threw Iceni tribespeople off their land. But they hadn't reckoned on Queen Boudica – she wasn't the kind of woman to let them get away with it.

REBEL VICTORY

Boudica led the Iceni tribe in a rebellion against the Romans. They were joined by warriors from other tribes who were equally fed up with the invaders. The rebel army, complete with horse-drawn war chariots, headed for the Roman fort at Colchester, which was the Roman capital of Britain at the time. Hungry for revenge, Boudica and her rebel army defeated the Roman ninth legion and destroyed the fort.

HARDOMETER

CUNNING: 7
COURAGE: 9
SURVIVAL SKILLS: 7
RUTHLESSNESS: 7

LONDON'S BURNING

Next, Boudica and her brave band of rebels headed for London, which was then a small trading settlement. She was hoping for a fight with the forces of Suetonius, the Roman governor of Britain, but he didn't fancy his chances – at least, not there and then. So instead Boudica laid waste to London, smashing and burning, then marched north and did the same thing in Saint Albans.

FINAL BATTLE

So far Boudica hadn't met with much opposition. But Suetonius was preparing his Roman forces, and marched them to meet Boudica. The two armies met somewhere in the middle of England (no one is sure exactly where). Boudica's army put up a strong fight, but they were outmanoeuvred by the Romans, who attacked with a hail of spears, then drove the British Army back and trapped them. Boudica's army was finally defeated. According to legend, Boudica herself wasn't killed in the battle, but took poison and killed herself to avoid being captured and shamed by her hated Roman enemies.

NAPOLEON

Napoleon Bonaparte led revolutionary France to war against the powerful countries of Europe, and succeeded – for a while.

HARD NUT RATING: 8

REVOLUTION AND REBELLION

The French Revolution began in 1789, the result of an unfair system in France that meant wealthy people lived in luxury while the poor starved. Napoleon was a 20-year-old French Army officer. He supported the revolution, and led his troops against French rebels who had joined forces with foreign troops in Toulon. Napoleon defeated them, and became a revolutionary hero.

NAPOLEON VS THE WORLD

Lots of European countries wanted to stop the Revolution, because they were worried it could spread – the people in charge liked things just the way they were. Brave hard nut Napoleon was the man to stand up to them. He was given command of the French Army and fought the Austrians and their allies, defeated them and forced them to make peace. But at the Battle of the Nile, British admiral Lord Nelson, defeated him.

HARDOMETER

CUNNING: 8
COURAGE: 8
SURVIVAL SKILLS: 8
RUTHLESSNESS: 8

INVASION PLANS

Napoleon wasn't happy with the way things were run, and took control of France in 1804 and made himself Emperor. He decided that invasion was the way forward, but was stopped from invading Britain at the

Battle of Trafalgar (Lord Nelson again). He was more successful with other chunks of Europe, and installed friends and relatives to run them, making France the most powerful nation in Europe. But then his army suffered a massive defeat when it tried to invade Russia – hundreds of thousands of French soldiers were killed by the Russians, or starved or froze to death.

SURRENDER AND EXILE

Napoleon had to surrender, and was banished to the island of Elba in the Mediterranean. The old ways began to return to France, and Napoleon simply had to do something about it: in 1815 he escaped from Elba, marched on Paris, and gathered an army. Things were going well . . . until the Battle of Waterloo, where Napoleon was defeated for the last time, by the British Duke of Wellington (see page 24). He was captured and exiled again – this time to a really remote island, St Helena in the South Atlantic. He died there in 1821.

TOMYRIS

Tomyris was a warrior queen who refused to be intimidated by the biggest empire in the world.

HAVING FRIENDS FOR TEA

Tomyris was Queen of the Massagetae, a hard-nut tribe who lived in Central Asia. According to an ancient historian, they had some unusual customs. Apparently when men got old they were killed and eaten by the rest of the tribe. It was considered a privilege to be eaten!

CYRUS THE CONQUEROR

In 530 BC, Cyrus the Great, ruler of the huge Persian Empire, realised he'd forgotten to conquer the Masssagetae, and decided to do something about it. His first attempt at grabbing the Massagetae lands was to propose marriage to Tomyris. She turned him down, so Cyrus prepared for invasion. He began building a bridge across to the Massagetae. Tomyris wasn't bothered and sent Cyrus a message, saying if he wanted a fight he could pick which side of the river to have it on.

TRICKY PERSIANS

The Persians played a sneaky trick – they left their main camp with a small number of soldiers to guard it, while the rest of the army decamped elsewhere. Massagetae soldiers, led by Tomyris' son, Spargapises, found the camp, killed all the soldiers, and started on the food and wine that the Persians had left for them. Then they all had a little snooze. That was when the Persian Army arrived and killed everyone except Spargapises, who they took as their prisoner.

TOMYRIS GETS CROSS

Tomyris demanded that Cyrus release her son, promising a big fight if he didn't. Cyrus ignored her, and Spargapises killed himself in shame. When Tomyris found out she was very sad, and completely furious. She led her army against the Persians – the mightiest conquering army in the world at the time – and won.

A GRUESOME ENDING

Cyrus was killed in the battle. The story goes that Tomyris dipped his severed head in an animal skin full of blood, saying that he could have his fill of bloodshed. Then she kept his skull as a drinking vessel. We don't know what happened to Tomyris herself – maybe she had many happy years drinking from her enemy's skull!

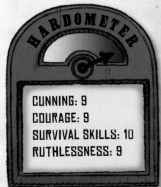

HARDOMETER

CUNNING: 9
COURAGE: 9
SURVIVAL SKILLS: 10
RUTHLESSNESS: 9

SHIHUANGDI

Shihuangdi had to do a lot of fighting, but eventually he united the different Chinese states into one country, and became its first emperor.

POWER STRUGGLES

When Shihuangdi became King of the state of Qin (pronounced chin) in 246 BC, there were seven states within China who were constantly at war. Shihuangdi decided that everyone would be much better off if all the states became one united China, with him in charge of the lot. Unfortunately, the leaders of the other states had similar ideas. By 221 BC, after nine years of fighting, Shihuangdi had achieved his ambition. He gave himself the name Qin Shihaungdi, which means First August and Divine Emperor of Qin. The name China comes from Shihuangdi's home state.

KEEPING IT TOGETHER

Shihuangdi wanted to make sure his united China stayed that way, so he made everyone use the same language, money, weights and measures. He changed the way the country was divided, too, so that the old regions didn't exist any more. And he decided his unified country should do some conquering – he added a large chunk of land to the south of China, the area that's now Vietnam.

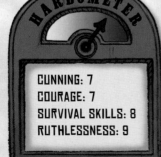

HARDOMETER

CUNNING: 7
COURAGE: 7
SURVIVAL SKILLS: 8
RUTHLESSNESS: 9

GREAT WALL

In the north, though, Shihuangdi didn't manage to conquer anything. In fact, northern invaders looked as though they might do some conquering of their own, so Shihuangdi had a massive wall built to keep them out. The wall doesn't exist today – another Great Wall of China was built much later, in the Ming Dynasty – but hundreds of thousands of workers died from hunger and exhaustion building Shihuangdi's wall.

ETERNAL WARRIORS

China's first emperor became a bit unhinged as time went on. He searched for the elixir of eternal life (he didn't find it), ordered all books to be burned (with a few exceptions – such as the books in his own library), and had hundreds of scholars buried alive. When he died in 210 BC, Shihuangdi was buried in an extremely impressive grave – a vast underground tomb filled with life-sized warriors and horses made from terracotta.

While Qin didn't succeed in his search for eternal life, his terracotta army lived for thousands of years.

CHOOSE YOUR WEAPON

You can't be a warrior without a weapon. It could be something as simple as a rock (for Stone Age warriors), or as sophisticated as a cannon. Below are a few choice weapons that have been used throughout history.

TREBUCHET

If you're a medieval warrior with a city to besiege, you need one of these. They're a bit like giant catapults, with a long arm that has a container at one end, and a heavy weight at the other. Simply place the missile of your choice in the container (rocks/severed heads/horse manure), let the weight pull down the arm, and fling the missile at your target. Perfect for battering city walls.

BOW AND ARROW

The bow and arrow was one of the first weapons to be invented and requires a lot of skill. They're an ideal choice if you're a member of a Mongolian horde, though you will need to be an expert horse-rider as well as an accurate archer. Longbows are the most effective (useful in the Hundred Years War) and can even beat crossbows if you're skilful enough.

WAR CHARIOT

These two-wheeled carriages have been around for thousands of years. If you're an ancient Egyptian warrior, or perhaps a Celt who wants the Romans out, this is a must for the skilled horseman. A team with an archer and deadly scythes fixed to the wheel axles of the chariot really show the enemy who's boss.

SAMURAI SWORD

If you really want to terrify your enemies, wielding a samurai sword should do the trick, especially if you're dressed in full samurai regalia. These long, curved, elaborately decorated swords are held with two hands.

GREEK FIRE

If you're a 17th-century Byzantine warrior and you want the element of surprise, you need Greek fire. Today, no one's sure what it actually was – maybe a mixture of sulphur, charcoal, quicklime and petrol – but it terrified the enemies of the Byzantine Empire because it was impossible to put out and even burned on water. It was thrown in pots (like hand-grenades) or shot through tubes.

CANNON

These powerful weapons replaced trebuchets for bombarding castles and cities, and are also useful in sea battles, though loading and firing heavy cannons can be a dangerous business.

CHARLEMAGNE

Charlemagne was a medieval warrior king who conquered most of Western Europe for the first time since the ancient Romans.

HARD NUT RATING: 8

FRANKISH KINGDOM

Charlemagne became King of the Franks in 768. At first he ruled with his brother, then on his own from 771 when his brother died. The Franks had battled the Romans hundreds of years before, then settled in modern-day France. Over the years, the Frankish kingdom grew as it conquered more and more territory, until in Charlemagne's time it covered most of what's now France, plus Belgium, Austria and a few other chunks of Europe.

SAXON WARS

Something was bothering Charlemagne: the kingdom of Saxony (now in northwest Germany), which he strongly believed should be part of his own kingdom. The Saxons disagreed, also very strongly. Charlemagne's war with the Saxons continued for more than 30 long years. There were 18 major battles, and many thousands of deaths – in 782 Charlemagne killed 4,500 Saxon prisoners of war in one go – and in the end, in 804, Charlemagne won. The Saxons had been quite happy with their own religion, but Charlemagne made them become Christians on pain of death.

HARDOMETER

CUNNING: 8
COURAGE: 8
SURVIVAL SKILLS: 8
RUTHLESSNESS: 8

THE FRANKS SPREAD OUT

The war with Saxony didn't stop Charlemagne getting involved in other fights at the same time. His father had helped the Pope fight the troublesome Lombards, and when a different Pope asked Charlemagne for help against the same enemy, he felt he couldn't say no. It also provided a great conquering opportunity: Charlemagne battered the Lombards and added Lombardy (now part of northern Italy) to his kingdom. Somehow, Charlemagne also found the time to conquer chunks of what's now Germany and Austria, as well as some of the land bordering his kingdom in the Pyrrenees. He gained vast new territories and enormous wealth.

HOLY ROMANS

Charlemagne helped out Pope Leo III in a rebellion against him. In return, Leo gave Charlemagne land in the middle part of Italy, and Charlemagne became Emperor of the Romans in 800. When he died in 814, Charlemagne had united most of Western Europe in the Holy Roman Empire.

TOMOE GOZEN

Tomoe Gozen was a female Japanese samurai warrior, who fought bravely and became a legendary heroine.

SCARY SAMURAI

Samurai were originally bodyguards for Japanese lords. They became a class of warriors, famous for their ferocity and the code they lived by, bushido, based on self-discipline, loyalty and honour. They looked absolutely terrifying with their elaborate armour and fearsome swords. Amongst the many male samurai, there were a small number of women. Tomoe Gozen is one of the fiercest and most famous, though it's impossible to tell which parts of her story are true and which are invented.

RIVAL CLANS

Tomoe Gozen took part in the Gempei War, fought from 1180 to 1185 between two rival clans, the Taira and the Minamoto. Tomoe went into battle alongside Minamoto Yoshinaka, her lord and possibly her husband as well, against the Taira. She was quite a woman: a brilliant horse rider, skilled in martial arts, an accurate archer, an excellent swordswoman, very beautiful, and as hard as nails.

ENEMY HEAD

In one battle, so the story goes, she defended a bridge single-handedly. In another, she cut off the head of a Taira leader who tried to drag her from her horse, then presented his head to Minamoto Yoshinaka. Yoshinaka was killed near the end of the Gempei War at the Battle of Awazu, but Tomoe Gozen is supposed to have survived it, although the Minamoto clan lost the battle.

A MYSTERIOUS ENDING

There are different stories about what happened to Tomoe Gozen in the end. One story says she became a concubine (a sort of second-class wife) of the enemy leader, and later became a nun. Another story says that after the Battle of Awazu, rather than face capture she committed seppuku, a gruesome method of suicide by plunging the samurai sword into the stomach. In another gruesome alternative ending, Tomoe Gozen found Yoshinaka's head on the battlefield and carried it with her as she walked into the sea and drowned herself.

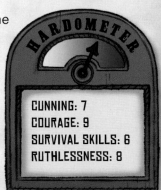

HARDOMETER

CUNNING: 7
COURAGE: 9
SURVIVAL SKILLS: 6
RUTHLESSNESS: 8

TIMUR

Timur was one of the most ruthless conquerors in history. His conquering career lasted nearly 40 years.

HARD NUT RATING: 9.3

TAKING TRANSOXANIA

Timur lived near Samarkand in Transoxania (modern Uzbekistan), which was ruled by a neighbouring leader. Timur was made minister of Transoxania under its ruler, Ilyas Khoja, but instead he joined forces with his brother-in-law, attacked Khoja and captured Transoxania. Then he had his brother-in-law assassinated. Timur was finally in charge.

CONQUESTS

Timur fought and conquered neighbouring states, and supported the leader of the Crimea against the Russians and other enemies by occupying Moscow and defeating the Lithuanians. But his conquering career really got going in the Middle East and Central Asia: over a period of about ten years he captured large chunks of what's now Iran, Iraq, Armenia, Azerbaijan, Georgia and Turkey, leaving destruction in his wake. Timur wasn't the sort of conqueror who appreciated beautiful cities and ancient sites – if it was in his way, he smashed it up.

HARDOMETER

CUNNING: 9
COURAGE: 9
SURVIVAL SKILLS: 9
RUTHLESSNESS: 10

THE GOLDEN HORDE

You wouldn't have thought he'd have time, but while all that conquering was going on, Timur was also fighting Tokhtamysh, leader of the Golden Horde (the western part of the old Mongol

Empire). Tokhtamysh was constantly invading land Timur had conquered, which made Timur very cross indeed. After a series of victories and defeats, Timur finally beat Tokhtamysh in 1395. While Timur was away defeating Tokhtamysh, revolts in Persia were ruthlessly crushed by Timur's troops, who destroyed cities, massacred the people and built gruesome towers from their skulls.

DEATH AND DESTRUCTION

Nowhere was safe. In 1398, Timur attacked India, reduced the city of Delhi to ruins, and used elephants to carry away tons of loot. His path of destruction included the city of Aleppo (which he destroyed) and Damascus in Syria, and Baghdad in modern-day Iraq, where he massacred 20,000 people. Timur was turning his attention to China when he was finally stopped, not by an invading army, but by a fatal illness. The vast lands Timur had conquered were divided amongst his sons and grandsons, who argued about the divided empire until it was finally reunited by Timur's youngest son.

ATTILA THE HUN

Attila led a terrifying army of Huns, the toughest of the tribes that fought the Roman Army at the end of the Roman Empire in the west.

HARD NUT RATING: 9

BARBARIAN HORDES

The Huns were barbarians, which at the time of the Roman Empire didn't necessarily mean uncivilised thugs, it just meant anyone who wasn't Roman. The Huns came from Central Asia and, like the Mongols they were skilled horsemen and absolutely terrifying in battle, shooting arrows and throwing javelins from horseback with deadly accuracy.

HUGE HUNNIC EMPIRE

In 434, Attila became joint King of the Huns with his brother, Bleda. They ruled together until Attila decided there was only room for one king and had his brother murdered in 445. By the time Attila ruled the Huns, there was a massive Hunnic Empire, covering great swathes of eastern Europe and central Asia. But Attila wasn't the sort of leader to leave it at that. The Roman Empire was divided into eastern and western parts, and Attila attacked the Eastern Roman Empire, which had its capital in Constantinople (modern-day Istanbul in Turkey), and demanded huge amounts of gold.

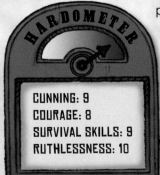

HARDOMETER

CUNNING: 9
COURAGE: 8
SURVIVAL SKILLS: 9
RUTHLESSNESS: 10

ATTACKS ON GAUL AND ITALY

Having caused as much trouble as possible in the Eastern Roman Empire, Atilla turned to the Western Roman Empire. In 451 and 452 he attacked Gaul (modern-day France and Belgium), but he wasn't as successful as he'd hoped. He was forced to retreat from Gaul when the Romans joined forces with the Visigoths and defeated the Huns. His attacks in Italy ended in disaster when his army was ravaged by disease. Still, he'd managed to do a lot of rampaging, destroying, and looting in the meantime.

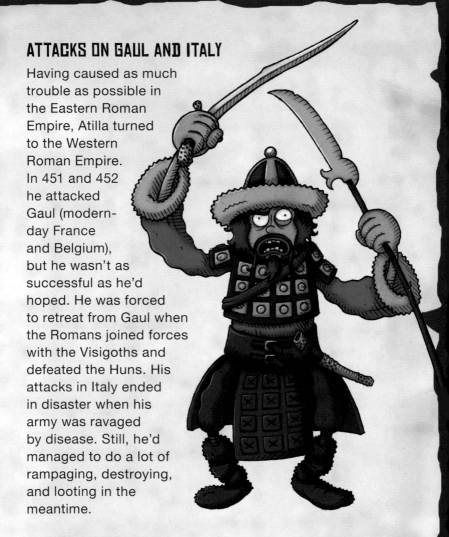

END OF AN EMPIRE

In 453, Attila's rampaging days came to an end: he died on one of his many wedding nights (Attila married lots of women), after having a nosebleed, or so the story goes. It might have been an illness that killed him, but it's also possible that he was murdered. After he died, his sons quarrelled over who should succeed Attila and the Hunnic Empire broke up.

WARRIOR QUIZ

Try this quiz and find out how much you know about the warriors in this book.

1. Which warrior united the Mongolian tribes and conquered an empire?

a) Attila the Hun

b) Charlemagne

c) Genghis Khan

2. Which queen defeated Cyrus the Great?

a) Boudica

b) Artemesia

c) Tomyris

3. Which Roman governor of Britain did Boudica fight?

a) Julius Caesar

b) Suetonius

c) Cicero

4. How long did the Trung sisters rule Vietnam?

a) Thirty years

b) Three years

c) Three months

5. Which country did King Piye of Kush conquer?

a) Egypt

b) Persia

c) Syria

6. Who was defeated by Julius Caesar at the Battle of Pharsalus?

a) Mark Antony

b) Crassus

c) Pompey

7. Who was exiled to the island of St Helena?

a) Napoleon

b) Alexander the Great

c) Charlemagne

8. Which empire was conquered by Babur?

a) The Ottoman Empire

b) The Moghul Empire

c) The Persian Empire

9. Which of these warriors died in battle?

a) Alexander the Great

b) Attila the Hun

c) Cyrus the Great

10. Who became the first Ming Emperor?

a) Shihuangdi

b) Hongwu

c) Taizong

Answers: 1 c, 2 c, 3 b, 4 b, 5 a, 6 c, 7 a, 8 b, 9 c, 10 b.

HARD NUT WARRIORS TIMELINE

761 BC

King Piye of Kush conquered Egypt.

559 BC

Cyrus the Great became King of Persia, and went on to conquer a huge Persian Empire.

530 BC

Tomyris, Queen of the Massagetae, defeated and killed Cyrus the Great.

336 BC

Alexander the Great became King of Macedonia, and quickly conquered a vast empire.

246 BC

Shihuangdi became King of Qin. Before long he had united China and become its first emperor.

PLACES TO CONQUER

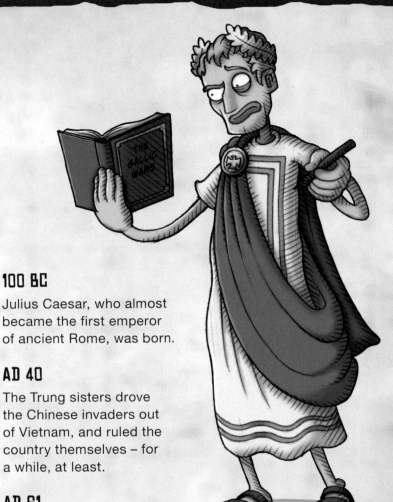

100 BC

Julius Caesar, who almost became the first emperor of ancient Rome, was born.

AD 40

The Trung sisters drove the Chinese invaders out of Vietnam, and ruled the country themselves – for a while, at least.

AD 61

Boudica, Queen of the Iceni people in Britain, died after her army was defeated by the ancient Romans.

434

Attila became King of the Huns, the most feared of the barbarian tribes in the dying days of the Roman Empire in the West.

768

Charlemagne became King of the Franks, and expanded his empire until it stretched into Italy.

997

Mahmud of Ghazni became king of the Ghaznavid Empire in Central Asia.

1185

Female samurai warrior Tomoe Gozen fought in the Gempei War in Japan.

1206

Genghis Khan united the Mongol tribes and became their 'Universal Leader'. Then he conquered the second biggest empire in the history of the world.

1328

Hongwu was born in China – he was a starving peasant, but went on to become the first Ming Emperor of China.

1336

Ruthless conqueror Timur was born – his empire eventually stretched from India and Russia to the Mediterranean Sea.

1412

Joan of Arc, the teenage farm girl who led the French Army, was born around this date.

1495

Babur became ruler of Farghana in Central Asia. He went on to found the Moghul Empire in India.

1769

British general the Duke of Wellington was born. His most famous victory was at Waterloo, when he defeated Napoleon, but he was also the British Prime Minister.

1804

French Revolutionary leader Napoleon became Emperor of France.

1829

Apache warrior Geronimo was born.

GLOSSARY

ASSASSIN Someone who kills people for political reasons

BARBARIANS Tribesmen who are seen by others as being uncivilized and primitive

BUSHIDO The way of samurai life

CAVALRY Soldiers on horseback

CIVIL WAR War between groups of people from the same country or state

CONCUBINE A woman who is in a relationship with a man, but is not his wife

DICTATOR A leader who takes total power and authority

DROMEDARY A type of camel that has one hump

DUEL A fight between two people, usually to the death

DYNASTY A series of rulers from the same family

ELIXIR A clear, sweet liquid taken as a medicine

EMPIRE A group of states or countries ruled by one leader or state

EXILE Banned from your native country

MASSACRED Brutally killed

PHARAOHS Leaders of ancient Egypt

PROVINCES Regions of land that belong to a country or empire

RAMPAGING Behaving in a violent, angry or excitable way

REBELLION A break away from (or resistance to) authority

RESERVATION A limited area of land where Native Americans live

REVOLTING Rebelling

REVOLUTION An overthrow of a leader

SAMURAI Military noblemen of Japan

SETTLERS People who move to a new area and set up home there permanently

SIEGE Surround a city or town with the aim of capturing it

SURRENDER To give yourself up (or give up control of something)

TACTIC A plan or system

TERRACOTTA A type of earthenware made of clay (the word means 'baked earth')

TREBUCHET A huge type of catapult

INDEX